TABLE OF CONTENTS

DANDELION LEMONADE

Fill a one gallon jar with water, 32 ounces clean, pesticide free, fresh dandelion blossoms, the juice of 4 lemons and honey to taste. Chill for several hours. Strain the flowers out. Dandelion blossoms are known to relieve headaches, cramps, backaches, stomach aches and depression.

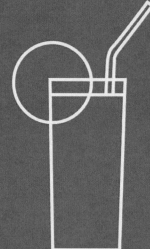

MY MORNING
SHAKE

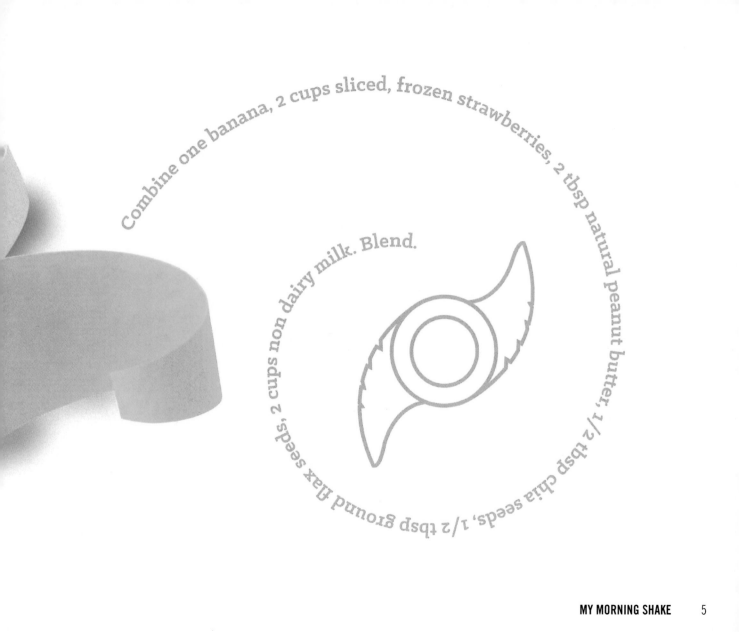

Combine one banana, 2 cups sliced, frozen strawberries, 2 tbsp natural peanut butter, 1/2 tbsp chia seeds, 1/2 tbsp ground flax seeds, 2 cups non dairy milk. Blend.

PEA HUMMUS

Combine in Food Processor: 1 cup raw, green peas, 1/2 cup chickpeas, 1 clove garlic, 1 tablespoon olive oil, 1/4 teaspoon salt, 1/8 teaspoon black pepper. Process until smooth for 5 minutes.

SUNFLOWER SEED BUTTER

Toast in 350° oven for 20 minutes
6 cups raw sunflower seeds with shells removed.
Transfer seeds to food processor while still warm
and process for 30 minutes till smooth and creamy.
Add: 1/2 teaspoon salt, 1 teaspoon vanilla.
Process another minute. Store in an airtight container.

CELERY STIX

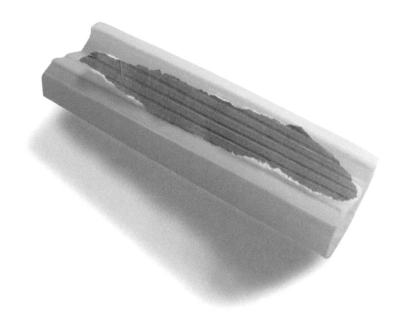

Slather celery with: peanut butter, hummus, goat cheese, cream cheese, cottage cheese or tuna for a snack.

BAKED SWISS CHEESE

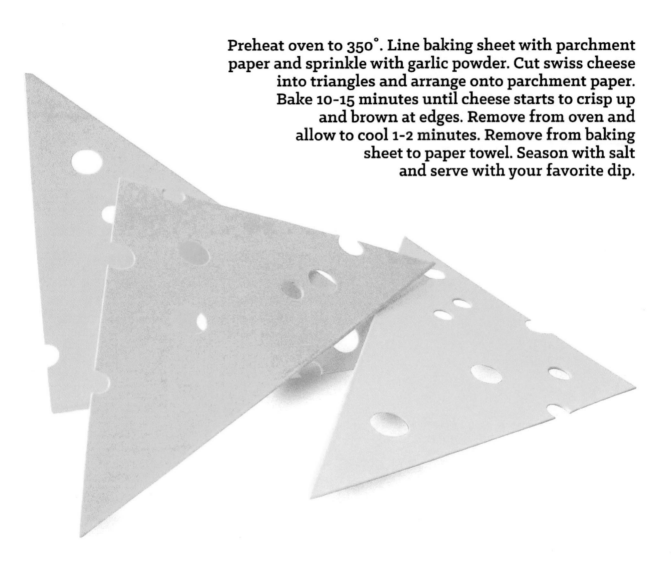

Preheat oven to 350°. Line baking sheet with parchment paper and sprinkle with garlic powder. Cut swiss cheese into triangles and arrange onto parchment paper. Bake 10-15 minutes until cheese starts to crisp up and brown at edges. Remove from oven and allow to cool 1-2 minutes. Remove from baking sheet to paper towel. Season with salt and serve with your favorite dip.

BEET CHIPS

Using a mandoline slicer
on the 1/8" setting,
slice 1 bunch chioggia beets.

Chioggia beets have distinctive red and white rings. Regular beets can be used also. Heat 3" oil in heavy pot and fry them in batches for about 2 minutes till golden. Drain on paper towels and sprinkle with sea salt while still hot.

CHIVE SOUP

Heat 2 tablespoons olive oil over medium heat.
Add 1 pound potatoes cut into cubes, salt and pepper.
Cook for several minutes before adding 2 cups vegetable stock.
Cover and cook for 20 minutes until potatoes are tender.
Add 4 tablespoons butter and 8 ounces chopped chives.
Blend mixture in food processor until smooth.
Add 2 cups milk.
Serve chilled garnished with chive flowers.

MY MOM'S COLESLAW

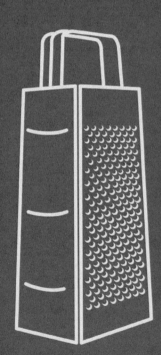

Grate one medium size head of cabbage into bowl.

Add one chopped small onion, salt and pepper.

Combine in pot two beaten eggs, 1/4 cup vinegar, 1/4 cup water and 6 tablespoons sugar.

Cook over low heat, stirring constantly, until thick. Remove from heat immediately.

Pour over cabbage while slightly warm, add 1 tablespoon mayonnaise.

Stir well.

Thinly slice 1 bunch of radishes
and pack into pint sized canning jar.
Top with 1 teaspoon red pepper flakes and
1/2 teaspoon whole mustard seeds.

QUICK PICKLED RADISHES

Brine: Combine 3/4 cup apple cider vinegar, 3/4 cup water, 3 tablespoons honey, 2 teaspoons salt. Bring to a boil over medium heat. Pour over radishes in jar. Cool to room temperature, close jar and store in the refrigerator.

LEMON/GARLIC VINAIGRETTE

Combine in a mason jar: 1/2 cup olive oil, 1/4 cup cider vinegar,
3 cloves grated garlic, juice of 1 lemon, 1 tsp thyme, salt, pepper,
1 tsp dijon mustard, 1 tbsp honey. Store in the refrigerator
and serve over your favorite salad.

SWEET ONION PIE

Preheat oven to 350°.
Combine and blend 1 1/2 cups crumbled crackers and 4 tablespoons butter.
Press into the bottom and sides of 8 inch pie plate. Refrigerate.
Melt 2 tablespoons butter and saute 2 cups thinly sliced sweet onions
with 2 cloves minced garlic for 12 minutes until tender.
Arrange onions and garlic in crust.
Beat 2 eggs, 3/4 cup milk, 1 tablespoon
chives and 1/2 teaspoon salt.
Pour over onions.
Sprinkle with 3/4 cup shredded cheddar
cheese and a pinch of paprika.
Bake for 35 minutes.

SHRIMP&
BISCUITS

Preheat oven to 400°.
Arrange onto a parchment lined baking pan
4 stacks of puff pastry, 3 layers high.
Cut a hole into the center of each and
brush with an egg wash. Bake 15 minutes.

Toss 8 large shrimp with 1/4 tsp crushed red pepper flakes,
1/8 tsp salt and 1/8 tsp black pepper.
Saute shrimp in 2 tsp olive oil for 2 minutes,
remove from pan and set aside. Add another tsp olive oil
to pan and saute 1 diced carrot, 1 diced celery stalk,
6 sliced mushrooms, 2 tsp fresh thyme for 10 minutes.
Add 1 tbsp olive oil and 3 tbsp flour and stir.
Add 1/2 cup dry white wine. Simmer for 2 minutes.
Add 2 cups milk and simmer 8 minutes. Add shrimp
back into pan, salt and pepper to taste.
Ladle the shrimp mixture in pastry bowls and serve.

TRI-COLOR PASTA

For 1 pound of homemade pasta the basic ratio is 2 cups flour to 3/4 cup liquid. The liquid consists of eggs, olive oil and vegetable juice or fresh herbs for added color or flavor. 2 cups flour, 3 large eggs and 2 tbsp olive oil.

Vegetable Pasta Variation:
2 cups flour, 2 large eggs, 1/4 cup veggie juice (beet, spinach, carrot juice, or tomato paste), 1 1/2 tbsp olive oil.

Mound the flour & make a large well in the center. Crack each egg into the well, followed by the remaining ingredients. Beat the eggs, oil and any other ingredients until well combined. Little by little, add the flour to the egg mixture and beat until all of it is incorporated. Mix the dough with your fork until it begins to take shape and you can gather it into a loose ball. Start kneading the pasta dough for 10 minutes until the dough firms up. When the dough is smooth and no longer feels sticky, shape it into a ball and cover with a kitchen towel to keep it from drying out. Let the dough rest for at least 30 minutes and shape into a ball.

Cut into quarters and work with each one separately on a floured surface.
Roll the dough as thin as you can get it. Dust with more flour to prevent sticking.
Fold the pasta sheet a few times over and cut to your desired width.
Spaghetti: 1/16 inch, Linguine: 1/8 inch, Fettucine: 1/4 inch
Dust the noodles with flour, shake them out and let them rest in
loose mounds on a towel while you roll out the remaining dough.
When all noodles are cut, drop them into a pot of boiling salted water.
Cook for 2 to 5 minutes, depending on thickness.

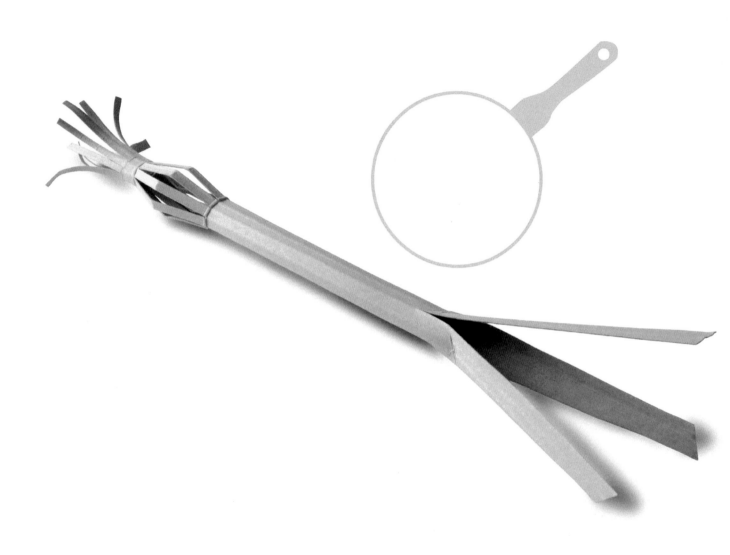

POTATO/SCALLION FRITTERS

Finely chop 12 whole scallions. Combine in bowl with 2 eggs, 1/4 tsp nutmeg, 1/2 tsp salt and pepper, 1/4 cup fresh bread crumbs and 1 1/2 cups leftover cold mashed potatoes. Shape into 4 patties and saute in 1 tbsp olive oil and 2 tbsp vegetable oil for 3 minutes each side till golden brown. Serve warm.

JERSEY TOMATO

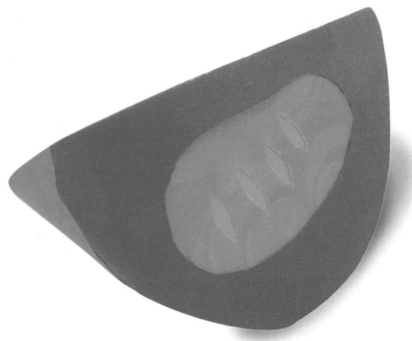

A tribute to my home state of New Jersey. There's nothing better than a freshly picked jersey tomato served many ways.

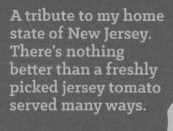

Whole, freshly picked from the garden and sprinkled with salt.

Sliced and drizzled with olive oil, salt and pepper.

Served warm with basil and melted mozzarella on top.

As a sandwich with bread, mayonnaise and cheese.

PORTOBELLO BURGER

Marinate several cleaned mushrooms for 2 hours in
2 cloves grated garlic, 2 tablespoons balsamic vinegar,
3 tablespoons olive oil, salt and pepper.
Cook the mushrooms on a medium high heat
grill for 5 - 7 minutes on each side.

Serve mushrooms on a bun like a burger with all the usual toppings.

THREE CHEESE RIGATONI

Cook rigatoni until almost al dente according to package directions.
Using a piping bag, fill cooled rigatoni with a mixture of 8 oz ricotta cheese,
4 oz soft goat cheese, 2 oz dolcelatte cheese, salt and pepper.
Layer filled rigatoni into a dish with your favorite tomato sauce
and fresh basil leaves. Top with grated mozzarella and bake at 350°
for 20 minutes or until bubbling hot.

COCONUT CUSTARD PIE

Prebake a 9" pie crust and cool.

For the filling: Whisk together 1 cup sugar and 3 tbsp cornstarch. Add 3 eggs until well combined. Scald 1 (13.5 ounce) can of full fat coconut milk. Add in a slow steady stream to the egg mixture while stirring constantly. Bring this custard mixture to a boil over medium heat, stirring constantly until you feel it thicken. Remove from heat and whisk in 1 tsp vanilla extract and 1 tbsp unsalted butter. Place a sheet of plastic wrap directly onto the surface of the custard and let it cool before transferring into the pie shell. Place in the refrigerator with the surface covered with plastic wrap. Chill for 3 hours.

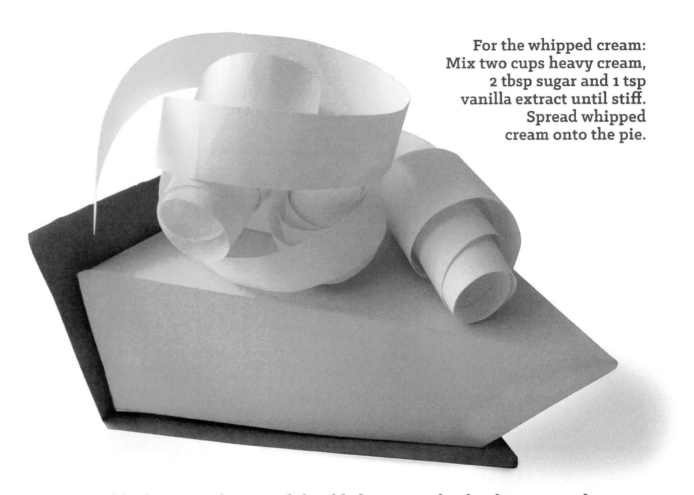

For the whipped cream:
Mix two cups heavy cream,
2 tbsp sugar and 1 tsp
vanilla extract until stiff.
Spread whipped
cream onto the pie.

Sprinkle the top with 1 cup of shredded coconut that has been toasted
for several minutes in a 300° oven until lightly browned and cooled.

PUMPKIN PIE

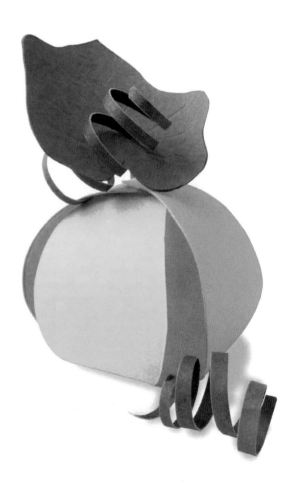

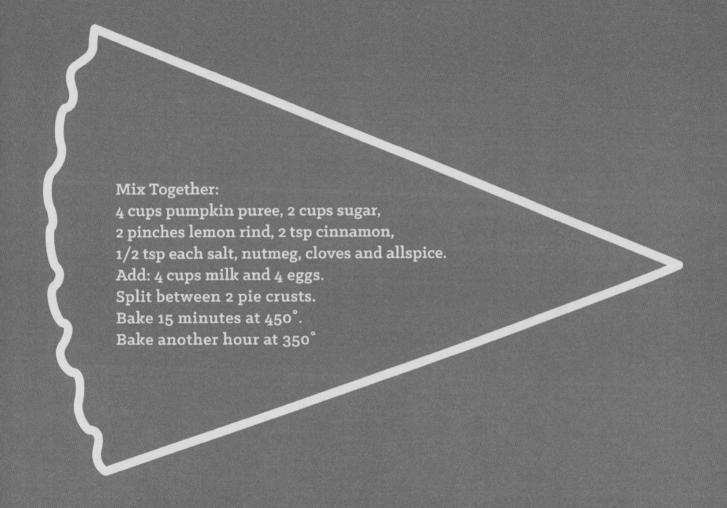

Mix Together:
4 cups pumpkin puree, 2 cups sugar,
2 pinches lemon rind, 2 tsp cinnamon,
1/2 tsp each salt, nutmeg, cloves and allspice.
Add: 4 cups milk and 4 eggs.
Split between 2 pie crusts.
Bake 15 minutes at 450°.
Bake another hour at 350°

Preheat oven to 375°.
Roll out your favorite pie dough and cut into 6 inch diameter circles.
Mix together four thinly sliced apples, 1/4 cup sugar, zest and juice
from 1/2 lemon, 1/2 teaspoon cinnamon, 1/4 teaspoon nutmeg,
pinch of ground cloves and 1 tablespoon flour.

APPLE HAND PIE

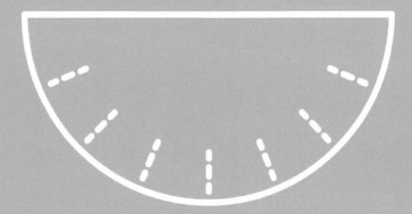

Place a spoonful of the apple mixture onto one half of each crust circle.
Fold crust over apples and pinch around half circle edge to seal.
Poke several holes in crust with the tip of a knife and sprinkle with "raw"
turbinado sugar. Bake for 25 minutes until lightly browned.

BROILED GRAPEFRUIT

with whipped cream

Preheat broiler and place four grapefruit halves onto foil lined baking sheet. Combine 8 teaspoons brown sugar & 1/4 teaspoon cinnamon. Broil 7 - 12 minutes. Serve topped with whipped cream.

Brush grapefruit with 2 teaspoons melted butter & sprinkle with brown sugar & cinnamon.

BROILED GRAPEFRUIT 45

MINT ICE CREAM

Combine 2 1/2 cups whole milk and 3 1/2 cups fresh "chocolate mint" leaves. Bring mixture to a gentle boil, cover and remove from heat. Steep for 30 minutes. Strain mixture, reserve milk and discard solids.

Combine 5 egg yolks and 2/3 cup sugar using the paddle attachment on the mixer. Beat on medium-high speed until very thick and pale yellow, for about 3-5 minutes. Return milk to a simmer. Temper the egg yolks by slowly adding half of the warm milk mixture to the egg yolks while stirring constantly. Add this new mixture to sauce pan with remaining milk. Stir consistently over low heat until mixture is thick enough to coat the back of a wooden spoon. Remove saucepan from heat and immediately stir in 1 cup heavy cream. Place an empty bowl over an ice water bath. Strain mixture through a fine mesh strainer into empty bowl and chill for at least 3 hours in the refrigerator.

Freeze custard in ice-cream maker according to the manufacturer's instructions. Store in an airtight container in freezer until ready to eat.

Pour some heavy cream onto "shortcake dessert shells".
The cream will soak into the shortcake.
Fill with sliced strawberries and top with whipped cream.
Serve.

CREAM

MOTHER-IN-LAW'S STRAWBERRY SHORTCAKE

MARBLED GINGERBREAD MAN

Prepare your favorite gingerbread and sugar cookie dough recipes.

Take a handful of dough from each and knead them together gently. Just enough to combine but not mix the colors into one solid color.

Roll the dough out and cut into gingerbread men with a cookie cutter. You'll get a swirly, marbled effect.

Bake according to the original gingerbread cookie dough directions.

VEGAN CHOCOLATE & BANANA CAKE &

Mix together for banana layer: 3 cups flour, 2 tsp baking soda, 2 cups sugar, 1 tsp salt, 2 tsp espresso powder, 4 tsp vanilla, 2 tbsp vinegar, 1/2 cup vegetable oil, 2 very ripe, mashed bananas, 2 cups water.

Mix together for chocolate layer: 1 cup non-dairy milk and 1 tsp apple cider vinegar and set aside for a few minutes. Add 3/4 cup sugar, 1/3 cup canola oil, 1 tsp vanilla extract and 1/2 tsp almond extract. Add mixture of 1 cup flour, 1/3 cup cocoa powder, 1/2 tsp baking powder, 3/4 tsp baking soda, 1/4 tsp salt.

Pour chocolate layer and then banana layer into a half sheet cake pan. Bake 35 minutes at 350° or until toothpick comes out clean.

Heat to simmer one 15 ounce can full fat coconut milk and 12 ounces dark chocolate. Remove from heat and add 1/2 tsp vanilla extract. Sit to thicken a bit. Pour over cake. Cool in refrigerator.

Preheat oven to 350°.

Cream together:
2 cups softened butter, 1 cup sugar,
2 tablespoons vanilla extract.
Add 3 cups flour and
2 cups crushed potato chips

Place spoonfuls of dough
onto ungreased cookie sheet.

POTATO CHIP COOKIES

Bake 15 minutes. Cool.
Dust with powdered sugar.
Makes 4 dozen cookies.

CARROT CAKE
dipped in white chocolate

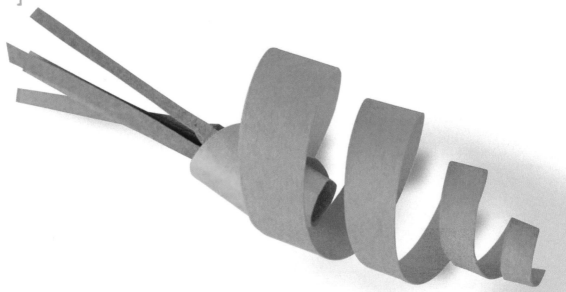

Combine 1/3 cup boiling water and 2 cups grated carrots. Add 1/2 cup vegetable oil, 1 tsp vanilla and 3 eggs. Combine and add 2 cups flour, 1 1/4 cup sugar, 1 1/4 tsp baking soda, 1 tsp each salt, cinnamon, nutmeg and cloves and 3 cups walnuts. Bake at 350° for 45 minutes in two greased and floured 9" square pans and cool. Spread between layers a mixture of 1 pkg cream cheese, 8 oz powdered sugar, 1/2 tsp vanilla. Cut into squares. Melt white chocolate and dip top, bottom and three sides of each piece of cake. Lay undipped side down on wax paper and chill.

lots of nuts!

CARROT CAKE DIPPED IN WHITE CHOCOLATE

CHILI PEPPER
CUPCAKE

Beat 3/4 cup unsalted butter and 1 1/3 cup sugar till fluffy.
Beat in 2/3 cup creamy peanut butter. Add 3 eggs, 1/2 tsp vanilla
and 1/2 cup sour cream. Add combined 1 3/4 cup flour, 1/4 tsp baking soda,
3/4 tsp baking powder and 1/2 tsp salt. Add 2 cups chopped roasted
unsalted peanuts, one finely chopped jalapeno and 1 1/2 tsp chili powder.

Bake at 375° for 13 minutes and cool.

Prepare chocolate ganache using 8 oz of spicy chili pepper chocolate bar and
1/2 cup heavy cream. Heat cream and mix with chopped chocolate and
1/2 tsp espresso powder until melted. Either dip cupcakes into ganache
while still thin or wait and let the ganache thicken and pipe onto cupcakes.

Top each cupcake with a piece of peanut brittle.

Peanut brittle: Combine 1 tsp chili powder and 1 1/2 tsp baking soda. Set aside.
Combine 1 cup sugar, 1 tbsp butter and 1 cup light corn syrup in pot over
medium heat. When dissolved, insert candy thermometer until it
reaches 275°. Add 2 cups salted peanuts to coat. Contiue to stir until
thermometer reaches 295°. Remove from heat and add the baking soda/
chili powder mixture. It will foam up. Stir and then scrape onto baking
sheet lined with aluminum foil that has been sprayed with non-stick
cooking spray. Allow to cool completely. Break into pieces.

S'MORES

- Salted Caramel S'mores: Add caramel and a pinch of salt.
- Strawberry & White Chocolate S'mores:
  Use white chocolate & add sliced strawberries.
- Lemon Meringue S'mores: Replace chocolate with lemon curd.
- Peanut Butter S'mores: Add peanut butter.
- Fruit S'mores: Add fresh fruit
- Coconut S'mores: Add toasted coconut
- Cookie S'mores: Replace graham crackers with cookies.
- Candy S'mores: Replace chocolate
  with the candy bar of your choice.

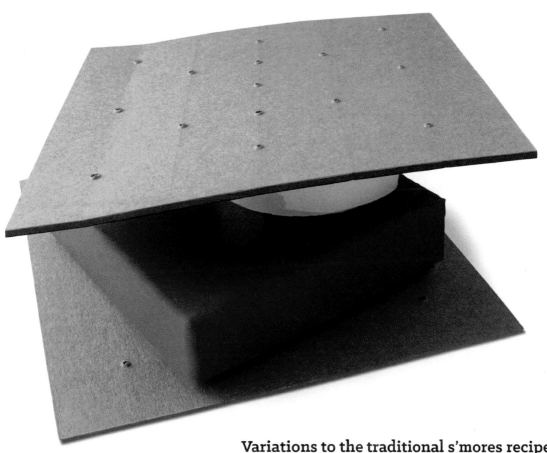

Variations to the traditional s'mores recipe using
Graham Crackers, Chocolate & Marshmallow.

THEY DRAW & COOK™

PAPER SCULPTED MEALS
by Joanne Frances DeWald

Conceived, designed and produced by
Studio SSS and Joanne Frances DeWald

STUDIO SSS, LLC
Nate Padavick & Salli Swindell
studiosss.tumblr.com

JOANNE FRANCES DEWALD
oftheforest.wix.com/oftheforest

Conversions

Common Measurement Equivalents

3 TS = 1 TBS = 1/2 FL OZ
2 TS = 1 FL OZ
4 TS = 2 FL OZ = 1/4 C
8 TBS = 4 FL OZ = 1/2 C
16 TBS = 8 FL OZ = 1 C
16 FL OZ = 2 C = 1 PT
32 FL OZ = 4 C = 2 PT = 1 QT
128 FL OZ = 16 C = 8 PT = 4 QT = 1 G

Oven Temperatures

300°F	150°C
325°F	165°C
350°F	180°C
375°F	190°C
400°F	200°C
425°F	220°C
450°F	230°C
475°F	245°C

Volume

1 TS	5 ML
1 TBS	15 ML
1/4 C	59 ML
1 C	236 ML
1 PT	472 ML
1 QT	944 ML
1 G	3.8 L

Length

1 IN	2.54 CM
4 IN	10 CM
6 IN	5 CM
8 IN	20 CM
9 IN	23 CM
10 IN	25 CM
12 IN	30 CM
13 IN	33 CM

Weight/Mass

1/4 OZ	7 G
1/3 OZ	10 G
1/2 OZ	14 G
1 OZ	28 G
2 OZ	57 G
3 OZ	85 G
4 OZ	113 G
5 OZ	142 G
6 OZ	170 G
7 OZ	198 G
8 OZ	227 G
9 OZ	255 G
10 OZ	284 G
11 OZ	312 G
12 OZ	340 G
13 OZ	369 G
14 OZ	397 G
15 OZ	425 G
16 OZ	454 G

Helpful Formulas

Tablespoons x 14.79 = Milliliters
Cups x 0.236 = Liters
Ounces x 28.35 = Grams
Degrees F − 32 x 5 ÷ 9 = Degrees C
Inches x 2.54 = Centimeters

Made in the USA
Coppell, TX
08 May 2021

55292688R00040